The New Novello Choral Edition

JOHN STAINER

The Crucifixion

A MEDITATION ON THE SACRED PASSION OF THE HOLY REDEEMER

for tenor and bass soli, SATB and organ
with hymns for congregational participation

Text selected and written by
Reverend J. Sparrow-Simpson

Revised by Michael Pilkington

Order No: NOV 072488

NOVELLO PUBLISHING LIMITED
8/9 Frith Street, London, W1V 5TZ

It is requested that on all concert notices and programmes acknowledgement is made to 'The New Novello Choral Edition'.

Es wird gebeten, auf sämtlichen Konzertankündigungen und Programmen 'The New Novello Choral Edition' als Quelle zu erwähnen.

Il est exigé que toutes les notices et programmes de concerts, comportent des remerciements à 'The New Novello Choral Edition'.

Cover illustration: title page of the revised edition of *The Crucifixion* (1915).

REVISER'S NOTE

The Crucifixion was first performed in St Marylebone Parish Church on 24 February 1887, and published by Novello the same year. In 1915 Novello issued a 'revised edition' in which 'the only alterations made are the substitution of the word 'plead' for 'pray' on pages 34 and 39 and the insertion of a new line in the hymn on page 39. Metronomic indications of the tempi have also been placed at the head of each number'. The alteration of 'woe' to 'pain' in the last bar of page 5 is not mentioned, but is clearly a correction of an error in the rhyme scheme. The new line on page 39 avoids an alteration of metre which would have caused problems in a congregational hymn. There is no obvious verbal or theological reason for changing 'pray' to 'plead'. However, these verbal alterations may have been made by the librettist, and have been retained here, with the 1887 words as footnotes. Since Stainer died in 1901 the authority for the metronome marks is uncertain; they are given here in square brackets, as are the few dynamic markings added in 1915.

The 1915 edition used the same plates as 1887. At some later date Novello had the whole work reset, though the plate number was only changed from 'No 8002' to '8002'. The layout of the organ part was adjusted to use both staves throughout; the notation of some chromatic passages was modified, and bar 46 of No. 2 was altered to match bar 13. No reasons are given in support of any of these changes, and the text of 1915 is followed here.

Michael Pilkington
Old Coulsdon, April 1998

NOTE

This revised edition of *The Crucifixion* follows the layout of the previous edition (catalogue number NOV070270) page for page, to allow this new edition to be used side-by-side with the edition it supersedes.

S-95

CONTENTS

Inscribed to his pupil and friend, W. Hodge, and the Choir of Marylebone Church.

THE CRUCIFIXION

Text
selected and written by
Rev. J.Sparrow-Simpson

JOHN STAINER

No. 1

Recitative: "And they came to a place named Gethsemane"

No. 2   The Agony

3

4

* woe, 1887

Je - sus and car - ried Him a - way, and de - liv - ered Him to Pi - late. And

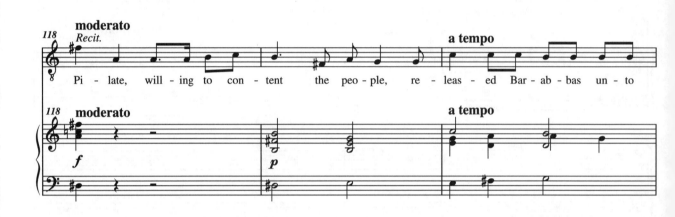

Pi - late, will - ing to con - tent the peo - ple, re - leas - ed Bar - ab - bas un - to

them, and de - liv - ered Je - sus, when he had scourg - ed Him, to be

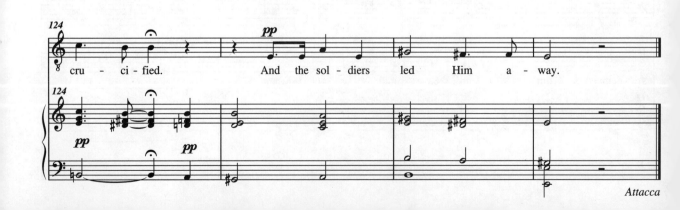

cru - ci - fied. And the sol - diers led Him a - way.

Attacca

No. 3   Processional to Calvary

14

100
fling wide the gates! the Sa - viour waits,
gates! fling wide the gates! He waits! the Sa - viour waits,
fling wide the gates! He waits! the Sa - viour waits,
fling wide the gates! fling wide the gates! He waits! the Sa - viour waits,
100
cresc.
104
fling wide the gates! fling wide the gates! the Sa - viour waits, To
fling wide the gates! fling wide the gates! the Sa - viour waits,
fling wide the gates! fling wide the gates! He waits! the Sa - viour waits, To
fling wide the gates! fling wide the gates! He waits! the Sa - viour waits,
104
Gt. [mf]
108
rall. cresc.
tread in His roy - al way; Fling wide the gates! He waits! the Sa - viour
cresc.
Fling wide the gates! fling wide the gates! He waits! the Sa - viour
cresc.
tread in His roy - al way; Fling wide the gates! He waits! the Sa - viour
cresc.
Fling wide the gates! fling wide the gates! He waits! the Sa - viour
108
rall.
cresc.

* bar 169, beat 2: S,T ♩♩ 1887

No. 4   *Recitative:* "And when they were come"

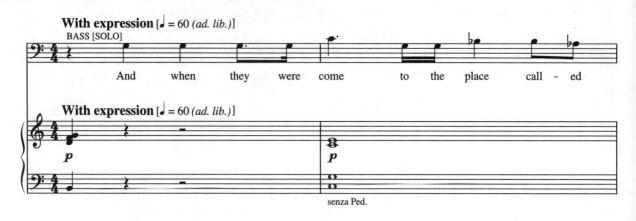

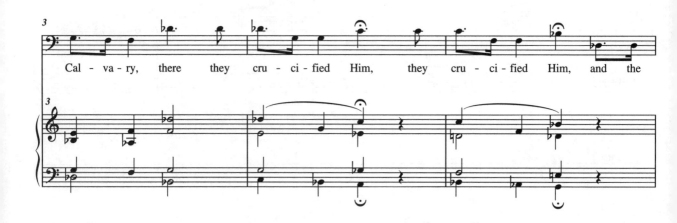

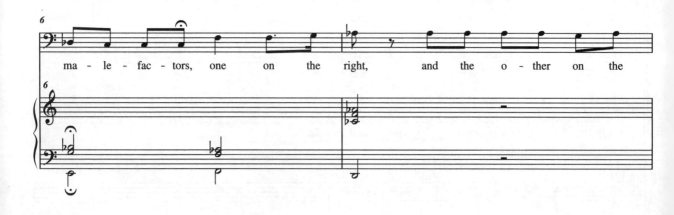

Attacca

No. 5

The Mystery of the Divine Humiliation

To be sung by the Congregation and Choir

Cross of Jesus, Cross of Sorrow,
   Where the blood of Christ was shed,
Perfect man on thee was tortured,
   Perfect God on thee has bled.

Here the King of all the ages,
   Throned in light ere worlds could be,
Robed in mortal flesh is dying,
   Crucified by sin for me.

O mysterious condescending!
   O abandonment sublime!
Very God Himself is bearing
   All the sufferings of time!

Evermore for human failure
   By his Passion we can plead;
God has borne all mortal anguish,
   Surely He will know our need.

This — all human thought surpassing —
   This is earth's most awful hour,
God has taken mortal weakness!
   God has laid aside His power!

Once the Lord of brilliant seraphs,
   Winged with Love to do His Will,
Now the scorn of all His creatures,
   And the aim of every ill.

Up in heaven, sublimest glory
   Circled round Him from the first;
But the earth finds none to serve Him,
   None to quench His raging thirst.

Who shall fathom that descending,
   From the rainbow-circled throne,
Down to earth's most base profaning.
   Dying desolate alone.

From the "Holy, Holy, Holy,
   We adore Thee, O most High,"
Down to earth's blaspheming voices
   And the shout of "Crucify."

Cross of Jesus, Cross of Sorrow,
   Where the Blood of Christ was shed,
Perfect man on thee was tortured,
   Perfect God on thee has bled!

No. 6   *Recitative:* "He made Himself of no reputation"

No. 7   The Majesty of the Divine Humiliation

Son of God, Thou Son of God. Glo - ry and

hon - our: Let the world di -vide and take them; Crown it's mon - archs and un -

- make them, But Thou,_____ Thou wilt reign.

Here in a - base - ment; crown - less,

poor, dis - robed, and bleed - ing; There, in

No. 8   *Recitative:* "And as Moses lifted up the serpent"

Attacca

No. 9 Quartet or Chorus *(unaccompanied):* "God so loved the world"

No. 10

Litany of the Passion

To be sung by the Choir and Congregation.

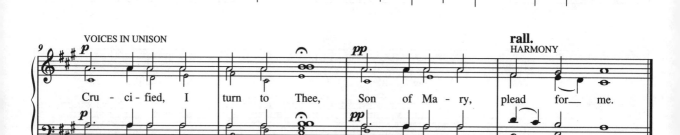

Cru - ci - fied, I turn to Thee, Son of Ma - ry, plead for me.

Holy Jesu, by Thy Passion,
    By the woes which none can share,
Borne in more than kingly fashion,
    By Thy love beyond compare:
        Crucified, I turn to Thee,
        * Son of Mary, plead for me.

By the treachery and trial,
    By the blows and sore distress,
By desertion and denial,
    By Thine awful loneliness:
        Crucified, I turn to Thee,
        Son of Mary, plead for me.

By thy look so sweet and lowly,
    While they smote Thee on the Face,
By Thy patience, calm and holy,
    In the midst of keen disgrace:
        Crucified, I turn to Thee,
        Son of Mary, plead for me.

By the hour of condemnation,
    By the blood which trickled down,
When, for us and our salvation,
    Thou didst wear the robe and crown:
        Crucified, I turn to Thee,
        Son of Mary, plead for me.

By the path of sorrows dreary,
    By the Cross, Thy dreadful load,
By the pain, when, faint and weary,
    Thou didst sink upon the road,
        Crucified, I turn to Thee,
        Son of Mary, plead for me.

By the Spirit which could render
    Love for hate and good for ill,
By the mercy, sweet and tender,
    Poured upon Thy murderers still:
        Crucified, I turn to Thee,
        Son of Mary, plead for me.

*1887 has 'pray' for 'plead' in the last line of all stanzas.

No. 11   *Recitative:* "Jesus said, 'Father, forgive them'"

No. 12   *Duet:* "So Thou liftest Thy divine petition"

No. 13

The Mystery of Intercession

To be sung by the Choir and Congregation

* Jesus, the Crucified, pleads for me,
  While He is nailed to the shameful tree,
  Scorned and forsaken, derided and curst,
  See how His enemies do their worst!
  Yet, in the midst of the torture and shame,
  Jesus, the Crucified, breathes my name!
  Wonder of wonders, oh! how can it be?
  Jesus, the Crucified, pleads for me!

  Lord, I have left Thee, I have denied,
  Followed the world in my selfish pride;
  Lord, I have joined in the hateful cry,
  Slay Him, away with Him, crucify.
  Lord, I have done it, oh! ask me not how;
  Woven the thorns for Thy tortured Brow!
  Yet in His pity so boundless and free,
  Jesus, the Crucified, pleads for me!

Though thou hast left Me and wandered away,
Chosen the darkness instead of the day;
Though thou art covered with many a stain,
Though thou hast wounded Me oft and again,
Though thou hast followed thy wayward will;
Yet, in My pity, I love thee still.
Wonder of wonders it ever must be!
Jesus, the Crucified, pleads for me.

Jesus is dying, in agony sore,
Jesus is suffering more and more,
Jesus is bowed with the weight of His woe,
Jesus is faint with each bitter throe,
Jesus is bearing it all in my stead,
† Pity Incarnate for me has bled;
  Wonder of wonders it ever must be!
  Jesus, the Crucified, pleads for me.

* 'Prays' for 'pleads' throughout, 1887
† 'With His agonised frame and his thorn-crowned head' 1887. See Preface.

No. 14

Recitative: "And one of the malefactors"

The Adoration of the Crucified

To be sung by the Choir and Congregation

I Adore Thee, I adore Thee!
Glorious ere the world began;
Yet more wonderful Thou shinest,
Though divine, yet still divinest
In Thy dying love for man.

I Adore Thee, I adore Thee!
Thankful at Thy feet to be;
I have heard Thy accent thrilling,
Lo! I come, for Thou art willing
Me to pardon, even me.

I Adore Thee, I adore Thee,
Born of woman, yet Divine:
Stained with sins I kneel before Thee,
Sweetest Jesu, I implore Thee,
Make me ever only Thine.

No. 16   *Recitative:* "When Jesus therefore saw his mother"

No. 17   *Recitative:* "Is it nothing to you"

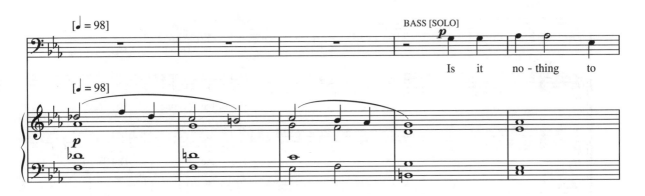

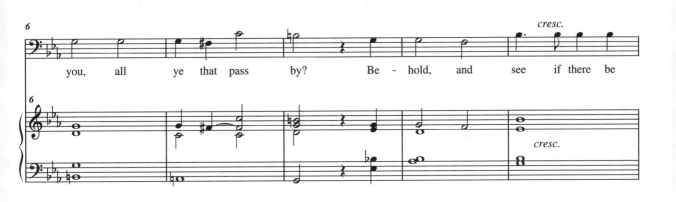

No. 18

The Appeal of the Crucified

[Ped.]

[senza Ped.]

50

No. 19

Recitative and Chorus:
"After this, Jesus knowing that all things were now accomplished"

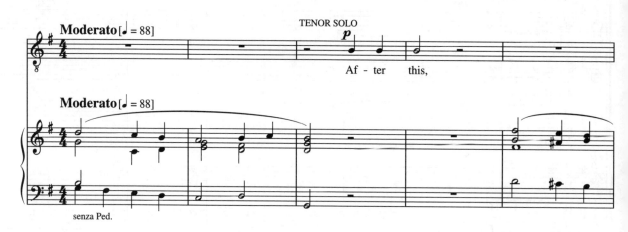

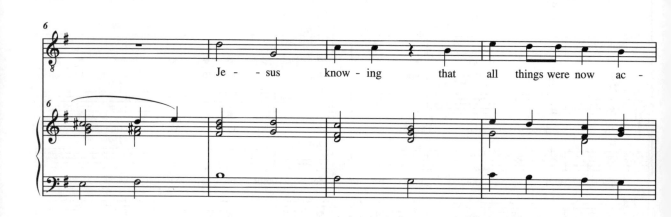

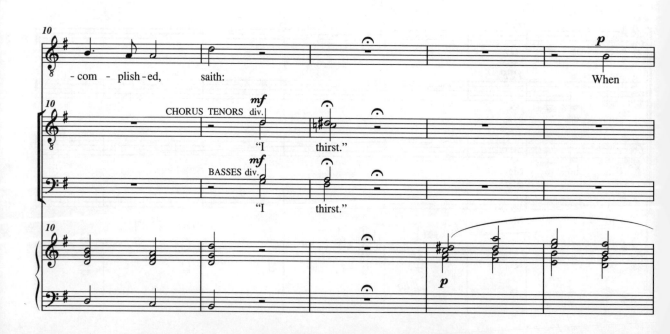

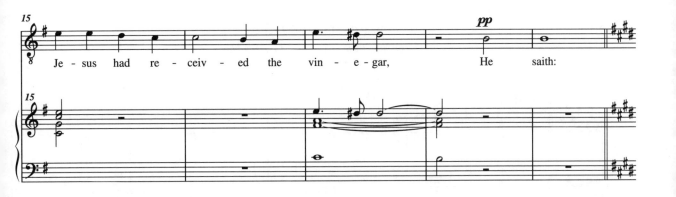

Je - sus had re - ceiv - ed the vin - e - gar, He saith:

Very slow

CHORUS
TENORS

"It is fin - ish - ed! Fa - ther, in - to Thy hands I com -

BASSES

"It is fin - ish - ed! Fa - ther, in - to Thy hands I com -

Very slow

TENOR SOLO

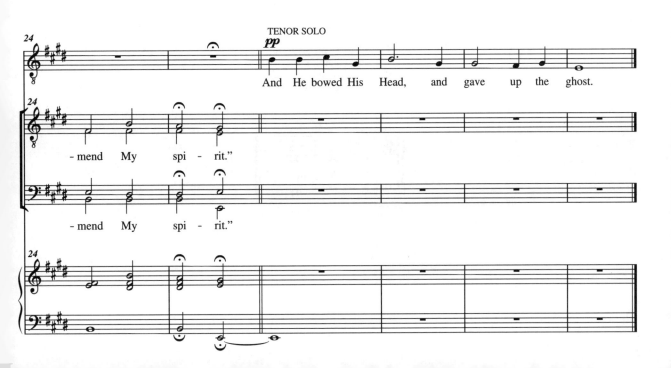

And He bowed His Head, and gave up the ghost.

- mend My spi - rit."

- mend My spi - rit."

No. 20

For the love of Jesus
To be sung by the Choir and Congregation

All for Jesus — all for Jesus,
　This our song shall ever be;
For we have no hope, nor Saviour,
　If we have not hope in Thee.

All for Jesus — Thou wilt give us
　Strength to serve Thee, hour by hour;
None can move us from Thy presence,
　While we trust Thy love and power.

All for Jesus — at Thine altar
　Thou wilt give us sweet content;
There, dear Lord, we shall receive Thee
　In the solemn Sacrament.

All for Jesus — Thou hast loved us;
　All for Jesus — Thou hast died;
All for Jesus — Thou art with us;
　All for Jesus Crucified.

All for Jesus — all for Jesus,
　This the Church's song must be;
Till, at last, her sons are gathered
　One in love and one in Thee.

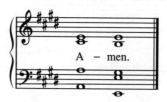

A – men.

Printed and bound in Great Britain by
Caligraving Limited Thetford Norfolk